Objects in Motion

Principles of Classical Mechanics

S. Galactic

α

S C U L   η

Ankaa

γ   β

P H O E

δ

κ   χ

Secrets of the Universe

Objects in Motion

Principles of Classical Mechanics

by Paul Fleisher

Lerner Publications Company · Minneapolis

For Lenette

The text for this book has been adapted from a single-volume work entitled *Secrets of the Universe: Discovering the Universal Laws of Science,* by Paul Fleisher, originally published by Atheneum in 1987. Illustrations by Tim Seeley were commissioned by Lerner Publications Company. New back matter was developed by Lerner Publications Company.

Lerner Publications Company
A division of Lerner Publishing Group
241 First Avenue North
Minneapolis, Minnesota 55401 U.S.A.

Website address: www.lernerbooks.com

Library of Congress Cataloging-in-Publication Data

Fleisher, Paul
Objects in Motion : principles of classical mechanics /
    by Paul Fleisher.
       p.   cm. — (Secrets of the universe)
    Includes bibliographical references and index.
    ISBN 0-8225-2985-8 (lib. bdg. : alk. paper)
    1. Mechanics—Juvenile literature. [1. Mechanics.] I. Title.
QC127.4.F57 2002
531–dc21   00-011960

Manufactured in the United States of America
1 2 3 4 5 6 – JR – 07 06 05 04 03 02

INTRODUCTION

Everyone knows what a law is. It's a rule that tells people what they must or must not do. Laws tell us that we shouldn't drive faster than the legal speed limit, that we must not take someone else's property, that we must pay taxes on our income each year.

What Is a Natural Law?

Where do these laws come from? In the United States and other democratic countries, laws are created by elected representatives. These men and women discuss what ideas they think would be fair and useful. Then they vote to decide which ones will actually become laws.

But there is another kind of law, a scientific law. You probably have heard about the law of gravity, for example. Where did that law come from? Who made it, and what could we do if we decided to change it?

The law of gravity is very different from a speed limit or a law that says you must pay your taxes. Speed limits are different in different places. On many interstate highways, drivers can travel 105 kilometers (65 miles) per hour. On crowded city streets, they must drive more slowly. But the law of gravity works exactly the same way no matter where you are. In the country or the city, in France, Brazil, or the United States, when you drop a ball, it will fall down. And it will always fall at the same rate.

Sometimes people break laws. When the speed limit is 88 kph (55 mph), people often drive 97 kph (60 mph) or even faster. But what happens when you try to break the law of gravity? You can't. Here on Earth, if you drop a ball a thousand times, it will fall down at the same rate of speed every time. It will never fall up or sideways, or just float in place.

The law of gravity doesn't apply just to people, either. All objects obey this law—plants, animals, water, stones, and even entire planets and stars. And we know that gravity stays in effect whether people are watching or not.

The law of gravity is a natural law, or a rule of nature. Scientists and philosophers have studied events in our world for a long time. They have made careful observations and done many experiments. And they have found that certain events happen over and over again in a regular, predictable way.

You have probably noticed some of the same things yourself. Gravity is a good example. When you let an object go, it will drop. Objects on Earth don't just float away. You know that from experience. Would you bet your life savings that a baseball tossed up into the air will fall back down again? It would be a safe bet. You'd be certain to win.

A scientific law is a statement that explains how things work in the universe. It describes the way things are, not the way we want them to be. That means a scientific law is not something that can be changed whenever we choose. We can change the speed limit or the tax rate if we think they're too high or too low. But no matter how much we want to float instead of fall, gravity remains in effect. We cannot change it; we can only describe what happens. A scientist's job is to describe the laws of nature as accurately and exactly as possible.

The laws you will read about in this book are universal laws. That means they are true not only here on Earth, but elsewhere throughout the universe too. The universe includes everything we know to exist: our planet, our solar system, our galaxy, all the other billions of stars and galaxies and all the vast empty space in between. All the evidence that scientists have gathered about the other planets and stars in our universe tells us that the scientific laws that apply here on Earth also apply everywhere else.

In the history of science, some laws have been found through the brilliant discoveries of a single person. The law of universal gravitation, for example, is the result of Sir Isaac Newton's great flash of individual understanding. But ordinarily, scientific laws are discovered through the efforts of many scientists, each one building on what others have done earlier. When one scientist receives credit for discovering a law, it's important to remember that many other people also contributed to that discovery. Even Newton's discovery was based on problems and questions studied by many earlier scientists.

Scientific laws do change, on rare occasions, but they don't change because we tell the universe to behave differently. Scientific laws change only if we have new information or more accurate observations. A law changes when scientists make new discoveries that show the old law doesn't describe the universe as well as it should. Whenever scientists agree to a change in the laws of nature, the new law describes events more completely, or more simply and clearly.

The laws that describe how planets move around the Sun are good examples of this. Astronomers once thought that the planets, the Sun, and the Moon all orbited the Earth in perfect circles. But new discoveries and improved measurements of the planets' paths forced two great scientists,

Copernicus and Kepler, to rewrite the laws that describe the planets' motion. The Sun doesn't revolve around the Earth after all, they realized. The Earth and the other planets revolve around the Sun! Once scientists realized this, they had to rewrite the laws that described the motion of the planets.

Natural laws are often written in the language of mathematics. This allows scientists to be more exact in their descriptions of how things work. For example, Newton's law of universal gravitation is actually written like this:

$$F = G \times \frac{m(1) \times m(2)}{d^2}$$

Don't let the math fool you. It's still the same gravity you experience with every step. Writing it this way lets scientists compute the actual gravitational force accurately in many different situations here on Earth and elsewhere in the universe.

The science of matter and energy and how they behave is called physics. In the hundreds of years that physicists have been studying our universe, they have discovered many natural laws. In this book, you'll read about several of these great discoveries. There will be some simple experiments you can do to see the laws in action. Read on, and share the fascinating stories of the laws that reveal the secrets of our universe.

CHAPTER 1

Planetary Motion

Every morning the Sun rises in the east. It travels across the sky in a great arched path. Every evening it sets in the west. The Moon follows a similar path. So do the stars. It looks as though these objects must be traveling in great circles around the Earth.

People have watched the sky and kept track of the paths of the Sun, the Moon, and the stars since the earliest times. And for thousands of years, astronomers thought that all those heavenly lights circled around us while the Earth stood still. After all, we can see the stars moving in the sky. Standing here on the Earth, we don't seem to be moving at all. Almost everyone agreed that the Earth was the center of the universe and that all other heavenly objects revolved around it in perfect circles.

But there was a problem. A few objects in the sky didn't fit into the pattern. Sometimes these objects seemed to stop, move backward for a while, stop again, and then resume their paths across the sky. Because these heavenly objects didn't follow a regular path like the stars, the Sun, and the Moon did, they were called *planets*, which means "wanderers" in Greek.

Astronomers plotted more and more complicated maps to keep track of the planets' strange wanderings. They drew maps with circles on circles on circles. But these complex arrangements still didn't solve the problem. The rules of science tell us that the simplest explanation is usually the best. It seemed unlikely that the heavens worked in such a complicated pattern. Astronomers began to realize that the whole system didn't make sense. They needed a simpler explanation for the movements of the stars and planets.

In 1543, the astronomer Nicolaus Copernicus published a new explanation. Copernicus believed that the Earth was also a planet. He said that the Earth and the other planets revolved in circles around the Sun. Many people found this new idea very disturbing. Human beings thought of themselves as being at the center of the universe. But Copernicus's theory said that the Earth was just one of several travelers around the Sun. It made the Earth seem less special.

Another reason why many astronomers disagreed with Copernicus at first was that the Earth doesn't seem to move at all. It feels as if the Earth is standing perfectly still. However, others realized that everything on our planet moves right along with the planet itself. The Italian scientist Galileo Galilei used a moving ship as an example of this. If a sailor at the top of a mast drops an object while the ship is moving smoothly, the object falls right to the base of the mast. The ship doesn't move out from under the object while it is falling. The sailor, the falling object, and the ship are all moving forward together at the same speed. Everything works just as if they were all standing still. Galileo argued that the same thing happens with the Earth as a whole. Everything is moving together at the same speed, and so we don't experience any motion at all.

After a while, most astronomers realized that Copernicus's idea was better than the old one. However, there was still a big problem. When astronomers tried to calculate the paths, or orbits, of the planets, their predictions still didn't come out right. The planets didn't follow circular orbits exactly the way the astronomers thought they should. To improve their predictions, astronomers began adding circles on circles again. And once again their maps became much too complicated. There still had to be a simpler explanation for how the planets moved.

In 1609, the Austrian astronomer Johannes Kepler finally found the explanation. Kepler's discoveries are known as the *laws of planetary motion*.

Johannes Kepler loved geometry. He believed that the circle was the most perfect of all shapes. Because he believed that the universe was God's perfect creation, he thought the planets must travel in perfect circles around the Sun. He was determined to prove that the planets traveled in circular orbits. Kepler spent year after year making careful calculations of the orbits of the planets. He used the very best astronomical information available. The information had been gathered by his teacher and employer, Tycho Brahe. Brahe was the most accurate astronomical observer of his day. There were no better measurements than his.

For years Kepler tried to make Brahe's measurements fit into a pattern of circles. But no matter how hard he tried, he just couldn't make them fit.

Kepler finally realized that the planets didn't move in circles after all. They traveled in ellipses, or oval-shaped orbits. The more he studied his information, the surer he was that it was true. In 1609, he published his *first law of planetary motion:* Planets travel around the Sun in elliptical orbits, with the Sun at one focus of the ellipse.

Unfortunately, we can't do a simple experiment to show this law in action. Experimenting with planets would be difficult. But we can experiment with drawing ellipses.

An ellipse is like a circle that has been stretched out in one direction. A circle has one center point. An ellipse has two. Each of the two points is called a focus (plural: foci, pronounced "FOH-sy"). To draw an ellipse, you will need a pencil, six pushpins, a piece of white paper, a piece of cardboard, and a piece of string about 30 centimeters (12 inches) long.

Pin the four corners of the paper to the cardboard with four of the pins to hold it down. Push the other two pins into the center of the paper, about 5 centimeters (2 inches) apart. Tie the two ends of the string together to form a closed loop. Slip the loop over both pins and stretch it out as far as it will go with the pencil. Next, draw with the

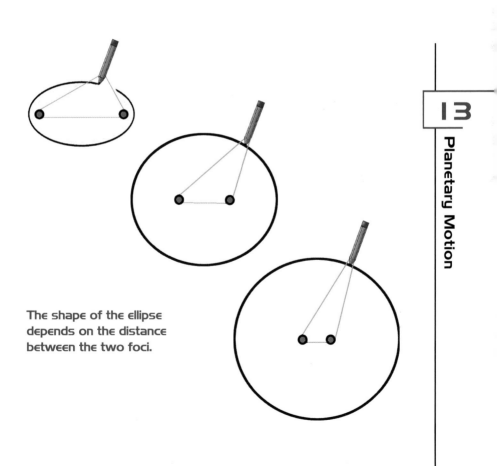

The shape of the ellipse depends on the distance between the two foci.

pencil, keeping the string tight as you move it in an arc. Draw half of the ellipse this way. Then move the pencil and string to the other side of the pins and draw the other half of the ellipse.

Look at the ellipse you have just drawn. If it were the orbit of a planet, the outer oval shape would be the planet's path. The two center pinholes would be the foci. One of the two pinholes would be the location of the Sun.

What happens when you change the distance between the two foci (the center pushpins)? How does the shape of the ellipse change when they are closer together or farther apart? Try moving the pins and drawing ellipses with several different distances between the foci.

You should discover that when the foci are farther apart, the ellipse becomes more stretched out. When they are closer together, it looks more like a circle.

The two foci of each planet's orbit are close together. So the orbits of the planets are almost circular, but not quite. It was this slight difference from a perfect circle that had given astronomers so much trouble. Once Kepler discovered that the orbits were oval in shape, tracking the planets' movements became much simpler.

Because their orbits are elliptical, planets are closer to the Sun at some times and farther away at other times. Planets' speeds also vary as they orbit the Sun. When they are closer to the Sun in their orbit, they move faster. When they are farther away, they move more slowly. Kepler wondered if there was a law that would exactly describe this difference in speed.

After more study and calculation, Kepler finally found it. It is known as the *second law of planetary motion:* A planet sweeps out sections of equal area in equal amounts of time as it travels along its orbit.

That may sound complicated. What does Kepler's second law mean? Suppose we mark Earth's position in its orbit on January 1 and again thirty days later on January 31.

We could then draw straight lines from those positions to the Sun, forming a pie-shaped wedge like this:

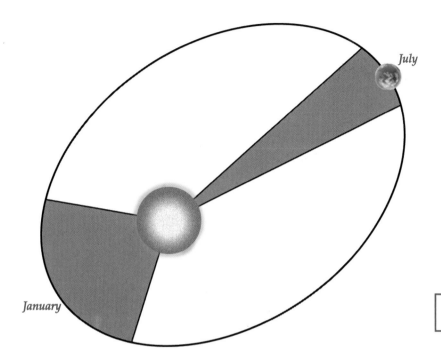

July

January

The two shaded sections have equal areas, even though the planet moves faster in January than it does in July. This drawing is exaggerated. Earth's orbit is much more circular, and the Sun and Earth are not drawn to scale.

That gives us an elliptical section of Earth's orbit. We could then mark another two positions, thirty days apart, on Earth's orbit. Let's say we mark July 1 to July 31. Again we can draw straight lines and form another wedge.

It happens that Earth is closer to the Sun during January that it is during July. Earth also moves faster in its orbit during January than during July. So the two thirty-day wedges have different shapes. The July wedge is longer and narrower than the January wedge.

Kepler's second law of planetary motion tells us that although the wedges are different shapes, they have the same area. That means that they cover the same amount of space. Kepler's second law is a mathematical way of saying that the closer a planet is to the Sun, the faster it moves in its orbit.

Planets farther from the Sun take longer to complete a single orbit than those closer to the center of our solar system. For example, Mercury revolves around the Sun once every 88 Earth days. Earth itself, farther from the Sun, takes 365 days to complete its revolution. Mars takes 687 days to circle the Sun. And Saturn, the most distant planet known in Kepler's time, takes 10,752 days. Kepler guessed that there must be some law that would describe this situation too.

After much additional work, Kepler found his *third law of planetary motion*. The third law says: The square of the time of each planet's revolution is proportional to the cube of its average distance to the Sun. This is a mathematical way of saying that the farther away from the Sun a planet is, the more slowly it travels in its orbit.

Here's a quick mathematical explanation of Kepler's third law. The square of a number is that number multiplied by itself. The cube of a number is that number multiplied by itself and by itself again. Let's call the time of a planet's revolution around the Sun R. Let's call its distance from the Sun D. Kepler calculated the value of the fraction for each planet in the solar system. The fraction looks like this:

$$\frac{R \times R}{D \times D \times D}$$

Kepler discovered that the fraction he got for each of the planets was the same. The relationship between a planet's distance from the Sun and the time it takes to revolve around the Sun stays the same, whether the planet is close to the Sun or very far away.

Why were Kepler's laws of planetary motion so important? First of all, they allowed astronomers to track and predict the motions of the planets more accurately. But the laws were even more important because they showed that planets follow regular, predictable patterns. That showed that it's not just objects here on Earth that follow natural laws. Other objects in the universe follow laws too. That was a new and very important idea. It let scientists expand their horizons tremendously. It told them that it was possible to study and understand the entire universe.

CHAPTER 2

Back and forth . . . back and forth. The chandelier in the great church swung at the end of a long chain. The Italian scientist Galileo watched carefully. He sat very still and counted his heartbeats as the chandelier swung from one end of its arc to the other.

A pendulum is simply a weight swinging back and forth on the end of a rope or chain. The chandelier swinging from the cathedral ceiling formed a kind of pendulum.

Galileo used his pulse to time the swings of the chandelier. He had to use his pulse because in 1581 no one had yet invented an accurate mechanical clock. But Galileo was about to make the discovery that would make the invention of a clock possible.

Galileo noticed that it didn't matter whether the chandelier took a wide swing or a very short swing. It always took the same number of pulse beats to complete its swing and return to its starting point. Galileo wasn't satisfied with just this one observation, though. He needed more information before he could be certain about how pendulums behaved in general.

Galileo tested pendulums with different lengths, different weights at their ends, and different arcs of swing. The fact that Galileo used experiments was very unusual in the 1500s. Scientists, or natural philosophers, as they were known at that time, often didn't use experiments to answer scientific questions. They used thought instead. If their idea seemed logical and sensible, they were satisfied that they had the correct answer. Galileo was the first great scientist to rely on experiments to test his ideas.

You can try some of the same kinds of experiments that Galileo did. All you will need is a sturdy string, several different fishing weights, and a watch.

Cut a piece of string a little longer than 2 meters (about 6 feet). Tie one end of the string to a support well above the ground. A plant hanger, a clothesline pole, or a standing lamp might make a good support for your pendulum. Tie a fishing weight to the other end of the string. Make sure it's free to swing without bumping into anything.

Make a chart like the one below:

Length	Weight	Width of Swing (S-M-L)	Total Time (10 Swings)	Time of 1 Swing (Total/10)

Measure the length of your pendulum and record the amount of weight you are using. Start with a small swing (S). Let the pendulum go, and carefully time exactly how long ten complete swings take. (One complete swing is the motion from the starting point of the swing to the other side of the swing and back again.) Then divide this total time by ten to figure out the time of a single swing. Don't forget to fill in your chart.

Then use a medium-sized swing (M). Time ten swings of the pendulum again and record your results. Finally, try a large swing (L). After you have tried different-sized swings using the same weight and length, change weights. Tie a different weight to the end of your string and repeat your experiments.

Shorten the length of your pendulum to 1 meter (about 3 feet), using the same set of weights, and repeat your timing measurements again. After you have finished timing those swings, shorten the pendulum one more time to about 0.5 meter (1.5 feet). Repeat your tests with the different weights and swings one more time.

Look at the chart. Notice the differences in the timing of the swings. Can you see what causes the difference in how quickly a pendulum swings back and forth? Are you surprised?

Galileo was. He discovered that the longer a pendulum is, the more slowly it swings back and forth. The amount of weight at the end doesn't affect how fast it swings. Neither does the width of the swing. The time it takes for a pendulum to swing depends only on its length.

This was a surprising discovery because it didn't seem to fit with common sense. Common sense would tell you that a smaller swing would take less time. And perhaps you would expect a heavier weight to swing more quickly. Galileo's experiment showed that, in this case, common sense was wrong.

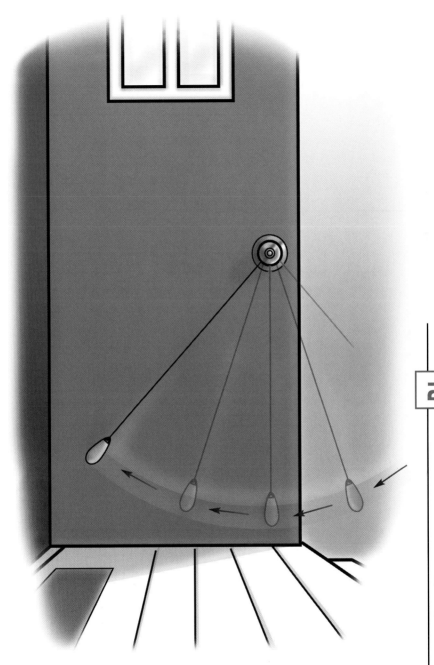

You can do your own pendulum experiments using a piece of string and a fishing weight.

After he completed his experiments, Galileo wrote a mathematical law to describe how to time a pendulum's swing based on its length. This *law of pendulum motion* soon turned out to be very useful. The Dutch astronomer Christiaan Huygens realized that if a pendulum of a certain length always swings at the same rate, it can be used to keep time. Around 1657, he used Galileo's law to create the first accurate pendulum clock. From then on, scientists could make careful and accurate measurements of time in their experiments. And, of course, the new clock had many other valuable uses.

Law of Uniform Acceleration

Imagine the following experiment: You carry two cannon-balls to the center of a high bridge. Both spheres are made of iron. Both are perfectly round. The only difference is that one cannonball weighs 1 kilogram (2.2 pounds) and the other weighs 10 kilograms (22 pounds).

Suppose that you drop both cannonballs from the bridge at exactly the same time. Which one will hit the water first? Will the heavier cannonball fall faster, or will the lighter one?

In the 1500s, natural philosophers knew the answer to that question. It was obvious! Of course the heavier object would fall faster. They knew this to be true because the Greek philosopher Aristotle, considered to be the founder of the natural sciences, had written about these questions many centuries earlier. Aristotle said that heavy objects fall faster than light ones. After all, consider what happens when you drop a stone and a feather. In fact, Aristotle believed that if one object was two times heavier than another, it would fall twice as fast.

For almost two thousand years, Aristotle's explanation was accepted as the truth. No one bothered to test it with an experiment. It just seemed sensible that heavy objects fall faster than light ones. But in 1634, Galileo once again showed that common sense isn't always correct. If you did the experiment described above, the two cannonballs would hit the water at almost exactly the same moment! In fact, Galileo discovered that objects fall at almost exactly the same rate no matter what they weigh. The only exception to this law is objects that are affected by air resistance, like feathers or sheets of paper.

If you want to convince yourself that this is true, why not try it? Use two different-sized fishing weights. Drop the two weights from a high place at the same time. If you drop the weights onto a hard surface, you should be able to hear them land at almost exactly the same moment. Be careful not to damage anything or anyone when you drop the weights!

Galileo didn't have a good way to measure the speed and acceleration of falling objects. They moved too fast to be timed accurately with his water clock, which measured time by collecting a steady trickle of water in a container. He needed a way to slow down a falling object so that he could time and measure it. So Galileo decided to experiment by rolling brass balls down long wooden ramps. The ramps had polished grooves that held the balls in place. Galileo timed the balls as they rolled down the ramps. He understood that the balls were still falling to the ground. But they were moving slowly enough to let him measure how far they traveled during each unit of time.

The experiment showed something very interesting. The balls seemed to accelerate (speed up) in a very regular way. A ball added the same amount of extra speed during each second. For example, if the ball traveled 1 meter (about 3 feet) during the first second, during the next second it would travel 3 meters (about 10 feet). That means that after two seconds the ball would have traveled a total of 4 meters (13 feet). During the third second, the ball would travel 5 meters (16 feet), so at the end of three seconds, the total distance would be 9 meters (30 feet).

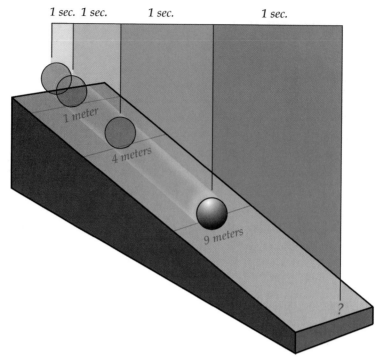

Galileo rolled balls down a ramp to study the acceleration of falling objects. How far will the ball travel in the fourth second?

See if you can figure out how far the ball would travel in the fourth second. What would its total distance be at the end of the fourth second?

During the fourth second, the ball would travel 7 meters (23 feet). And at the end of the fourth second, the ball would have traveled a total of 16 meters (52 feet).

Incidentally, the metric system of measurement wasn't created until the late 1700s. Galileo couldn't have actually used meters or grams as his measuring units. He used other units that were common in his time.

Galileo tried his experiment with the wooden track held at a very shallow angle. Then he repeated his procedure using steeper angles. Naturally the balls accelerated faster on the steeper tracks. But one thing didn't change: The amount of acceleration was always constant. The balls always added the same amount of extra speed each second.

Galileo realized that if the ramp was lifted all the way up to vertical, the balls would still accelerate in a regular, uniform way. Of course, if the track were vertical, the balls would actually be falling freely. That was the evidence Galileo needed for his law of falling objects. Because the acceleration of falling objects stays constant, this law is usually called the *law of uniform acceleration.* The law says that falling objects accelerate at a uniform rate. As long as air resistance is excluded, the rate is the same no matter what the weight of the object.

Just how fast do objects fall here on Earth? Galileo didn't determine that in his experiments, but later scientists did. They found that falling objects accelerate at 9.8 meters (32 feet) per second. That means that at the end of each second, an object is falling 9.8 meters per second faster than it did the second before.

Let's see what happens to an actual falling object. To make our calculations a little easier, let's round off the rate of acceleration from 9.8 meters per second to 10 meters (about 33 feet) per second.

Let's imagine dropping one of the cannonballs again, this time from a very high tower. An object that is dropped starts out with no velocity (movement in a specific direction) at all. When we first let go, the cannonball's velocity is 0. At the end of the first second, it has accelerated to a velocity of 10 meters per second. If we take an average of the velocities at the beginning and end of the first second, (0 + 10)/2, it's easy to see that during that second, the cannonball falls a total of 5 meters (16 feet).

At the end of two seconds, the cannonball has accelerated to 20 meters (66 feet) per second. It has also fallen another 15 meters (49 feet)—(10+20)/2. It has fallen a total of 20 meters in two seconds.

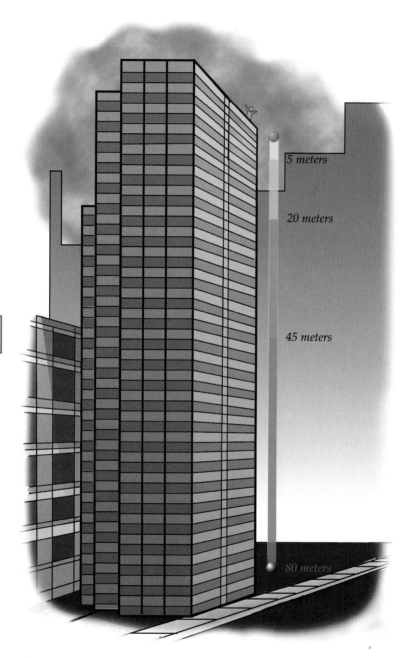

5 meters

20 meters

45 meters

80 meters

A cannonball moves faster and faster as it falls from a high tower.

At the end of the third second, the cannonball is falling at 30 meters (98 feet) per second. It has fallen another 25 meters (82 feet), for a total of 45 meters (about 148 feet) in three seconds.

At the end of the fourth second, our object is falling at 40 meters (130 feet) per second and has dropped another 35 meters (110 feet). At the end of four seconds, it will have fallen a total of 80 meters (260 feet).

As you can see, the cannonball is falling faster and faster each second. It will continue to accelerate until it hits the ground or until it is going so fast that the resistance of the air won't allow it to speed up any further.

Is Galileo's law true for every falling object? If you could take away air resistance, would a feather really fall just as fast as a heavy piece of metal? During Galileo's time, scientists didn't know how to remove all the air from a container to create a vacuum. But a few years after his death, a method for creating a vacuum was developed. Scientists then conducted an experiment to see if Galileo was right. They placed a feather and a gold coin together in a vacuum chamber. When they were released from the top of the chamber, they fell to the bottom at the same rate. Galileo's law was proved true.

Galileo made another important discovery about falling objects. He realized that projectiles (like cannonballs or baseballs) also follow his law of falling objects. He discovered that the motion of objects moving through the air can

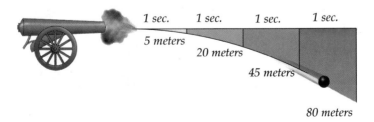

A cannonball follows Galileo's law of uniform acceleration while traveling forward at the same time.

be broken up into two parts. A projectile moves through the air sideways at a certain speed. But at the same time, it also falls down like any other falling object. And as time passes, its downward motion accelerates. If you shot a cannonball horizontally from the same tower from which we imagined dropping it earlier, its path would look like the one on the previous page.

Of course, the cannonball would travel much farther sideways. But it would still fall to the ground at the same rate as any other object. If you dropped one cannonball and fired another horizontally at the same time, they would both hit the ground at the same time!

Because he was the first scientist to prove his theories by actually doing experiments, Galileo is considered the founder of modern experimental science. But this great man did much more than study pendulums and falling objects. He also used the first telescope to make many great astronomical discoveries. He found that the Moon has features such as craters and "seas." He discovered that Jupiter is circled by moons of its own. He discovered that the Milky Way is made up of millions of stars. He was an important supporter of the theory that the Earth circles the Sun and was even arrested and put on trial for that belief! For these and many other discoveries, historians consider Galileo one of the greatest scientists who ever lived.

CHAPTER 3

Newton's Three Laws of Motion

It's a little after dawn on a warm Florida morning. On a huge concrete platform supported by a towering steel gantry, the space shuttle stands ready for takeoff. White plumes of vapor stream from vents in the smooth metal skin of the orbiter. Everything is quiet. Then suddenly a tremendous shower of flame erupts from the shuttle's engines. Gradually at first, then faster and faster, the gigantic but graceful craft roars into the sky.

The space shuttle is a miracle of technology. It is built with hundreds of special materials and equipped with the most effective life-support systems the National Aeronautic and Space Administration (NASA) can devise. But the natural laws that explain how the shuttle takes off, moves through the Earth's atmosphere, and orbits the Earth were discovered by the man who may have been the greatest scientist who ever lived—Sir Isaac Newton. When the space shuttle leaps into orbit, or when anything else in our universe moves, it moves according to the laws that Newton discovered and wrote down in the late 1600s.

The universe is filled with moving objects. Wheels roll, birds and planes fly, trees sway in the breeze. Basketballs bounce, kites soar, boats sail, and people walk. Earth and the other planets in the solar system move. So do the Moon, the Sun, other stars, and even galaxies. What do all the various motions in the universe have in common? Are there any rules to describe how and why objects move?

The study of how things move is called mechanics. Galileo studied mechanics when he experimented with falling objects. But it was the English scientist Isaac Newton who made the most complete discoveries about moving objects.

Think about what happens when a ball is rolled down a ramp onto a perfectly flat surface. It continues to roll, although after a while, it will slow to a stop. Early natural philosophers, followers of Aristotle, believed that the ball would need a continuous force pushing on it to keep it rolling. They thought that when the force was "used up," the ball would stop rolling.

Galileo realized that once a ball starts rolling, no more force is needed to keep it rolling. Galileo also realized that it is air resistance and friction (the rubbing of one object against another) that finally make it stop.

What if there was no friction or air resistance? What if there was nothing to slow the ball down once it started moving? Newton realized that unless some force acted to slow the ball down, it would continue on forever!

Suppose we place our ball on a perfectly flat surface and steady it so that it is perfectly still. Unless we use some kind of force, like a push or a puff of air, the ball will stay perfectly still. It will never move by itself.

Newton understood that an object will change its motion only if it is acted upon by a force. Otherwise, its motion will be unchanged. If it is moving, it will continue to move in the same direction. And if it is standing still, it will remain still. That is *Newton's first law of motion*. It is usually stated this way: An object in motion continues in motion and an object at rest remains at rest unless acted upon by a force.

This law is often called the *law of inertia*. Inertia is simply the scientific term for matter's property of continuing its motion (or lack of motion) until acted upon by some force. This property of inertia is what is described in Newton's first law.

You can see Newton's first law in action in the following demonstration. Get a drinking glass, a quarter, and a playing card. Place the card over the mouth of the glass and put the quarter in the middle of the card. Thanks to the law of inertia, it is possible to get the quarter into the glass without touching it. Simply flick the edge of the card with your fingernail. The card will go flying out, while the quarter will fall into the glass.

The trick works because an object at rest (the coin) remains at rest unless acted upon by a force. Your finger provides enough force to make the card move. But a playing card is slippery and doesn't create much friction against the coin as it is flicked away. That means there isn't enough force acting on the heavy coin to get it moving very fast. As a result, the coin falls into the glass as the card is removed.

The famous trick in which a tablecloth is pulled off a table, leaving all the dishes, silverware, and glassware in place, works exactly the same way. When the magician snaps the tablecloth away, all the dishes are at rest. Because of Newton's first law, they tend to remain at rest. The rapidly moving tablecloth doesn't produce enough force to move the dishes very much, and so they stay on the table. By the way, please don't try this trick at home. It takes lots of skill, heavy dishes, and a very slick tablecloth.

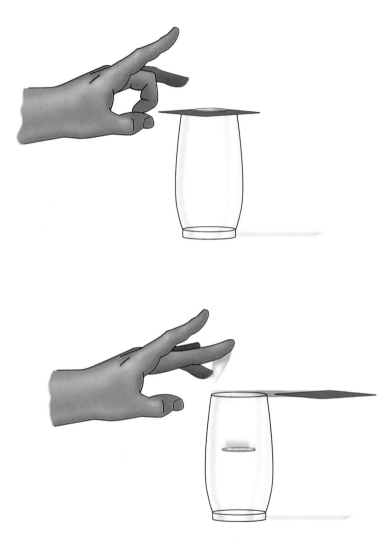

When you flick the card, the coin will fall into the glass.

Objects moving in space have no air resistance or friction to slow them down. According to Newton's first law, they should continue moving through space in a straight line forever. And that is exactly what happens. The *Voyager* satellites were launched into space in 1977. They carry messages of greeting from the people of our planet.

Their rocket engines stopped burning long ago. But the *Voyagers* are still traveling through space, farther and farther from the Earth. They will continue on their journeys for millions of years, until something or someone stops them.

Newton's second law of motion tells us how an object's motion changes when a force acts on it. To explain it clearly, we need to define two terms. Mass is the amount of matter or substance an object is made of. Notice that mass is not the same thing as weight. Acceleration is any change in the motion of an object. It can be a change in speed (either slower or faster) or a change in direction. As Newton's first law tells us, an object can't accelerate unless a force is applied to it.

Let's consider a situation from everyday life. Suppose your family's car has run out of gas on a level road. Up ahead is a gas station. All you have to do is push your car there.

One thing you certainly know is that the harder you push, the faster your car will roll. If only one passenger pushes against the back of the car, the car may start rolling, but it will move very slowly. And that one person will have to work very hard. But if three or four people push, the car will move much more easily. Why? Because four people can provide much greater force than one can. The greater the force applied to an object, the more it will accelerate.

Would it make a difference if your car were a small, lightweight compact or a heavy luxury sedan? Which would be easier to push? The smaller car would move more easily, of course. The more mass an object has, the more force is needed to make it accelerate. A luxury car has much more mass than a little economy model, so it takes more effort to overcome its inertia and get it moving.

So, the acceleration (or change in motion) of an object depends on two things: the mass of the object and the amount of force applied. The more force that is used, the greater the acceleration. The more mass to be moved, the less acceleration you will get with an equal amount of force.

These are the two ideas of Newton's second law of motion. The second law of motion is often known as the *law of acceleration.* It is usually stated like this: The acceleration of an object is directly proportional to the force applied to the object and inversely proportional to the mass of the object.

Before we go on, it's important to understand what directly proportional and inversely proportional mean. They are not as difficult as they may sound.

If two measurements are directly proportional, then when one increases, the other increases too. For example, if you are driving at 80 kilometers (50 miles) per hour, the distance you cover is directly proportional to the amount of time you drive. As time increases, so does distance. The longer you drive, the farther you go.

In the example of the stalled car, the greater the force used to push it, the more the car will accelerate. Acceleration is directly proportional to the amount of force being used.

If two measurements are inversely proportional, then as one increases, the other decreases. For example, if you are taking a trip of 100 miles (160 kilometers), the time of the trip will be inversely proportional to the speed that you drive. The faster you drive, the shorter the time of the trip. As the speed increases, the time decreases.

In the example of the stalled car, the more massive the car is, the less it will accelerate when we push it. Acceleration is inversely proportional to the amount of mass being accelerated.

The law of acceleration can be written as a simple equation:

$$\text{acceleration} = \frac{\text{force}}{\text{mass}} \quad \text{or} \quad a = \frac{f}{m}$$

To calculate the acceleration of an object, we need to know

the mass of the object and the amount of force applied to it. Notice that acceleration is written as a fraction. Force is the numerator and mass is the denominator. When we increase the amount of force (in our example, pushing with more people), the numerator of the fraction is larger. So the value of our fraction gets larger too. More force gives more acceleration.

If we increase the amount of mass (pushing a larger car, in our example), the denominator of the fraction gets larger. That means the value of the fraction gets smaller. So more mass will result in less acceleration, if the amount of force stays the same. That's why NASA is so careful about keeping everything in its spacecraft as light and small as possible. Larger, heavier spacecraft need more fuel and bigger engines to accelerate them into orbit.

If both sides of this equation are multiplied by m, this same law can be rewritten this way:

$$\text{force} = \text{mass} \times \text{acceleration} \quad \text{or} \quad f = m \times a$$

Newton's second law is most often written this way. It tells us that the force used to move an object (f) can be calculated by multiplying the mass of the object (m) times the amount of acceleration given to the object (a).

It also tells us that the faster an object is accelerated, or the larger it is, the more force it exerts. That should agree with your experiences in daily life. Think about playing a game of dodgeball. A ball thrown very hard will sting much more when it hits you than one that is tossed gently. The faster-moving ball has more force. A heavier ball will hurt more than a light one when it hits you, if they are thrown with the same speed. The ball with more mass has more force.

We can see examples of the second law of motion in action everywhere. When a batter swings and hits a baseball, the bat applies a force to the ball, changing its speed and direction. How far the ball goes depends on how much force is in the swing of the bat. Construction workers apply force as they move the steel girders they use to build skyscrapers and bridges. The more massive the girder, the more force needed to move it. The law explains why freight trains and jet airliners need such huge, powerful engines. It takes a tremendous amount of force to get all that mass moving!

Let's look at *Newton's third law of motion.* Picture a man paddling a canoe across a lake. Each time he takes a stroke with his paddle, he pushes some water toward the stern (rear) of the canoe. Each time he pushes this water backward, the canoe moves forward. Newton's third law of motion is known as the *law of action and reaction.* It is usually stated like this: For every action, there is an equal and opposite reaction.

As our canoeist paddles across the lake, he is pushing the water behind him with his paddle. That is the action. The reaction is the canoe moving forward in the water, with the same amount of force that the paddler used in his stroke.

Newton's third law describes why a rifle recoils, or "kicks," when it is fired. As the bullet fires forward out of the gun barrel (action), the force of the reaction pushes the gun backward against the shooter's shoulder.

Whenever you see a rocket or jet take off, you are seeing Newton's third law in action. When a rocket or jet engine is ignited, a tremendous amount of force is generated by the hot gases pouring out toward the rear of the vehicle. Newton's third law tells us that there must be an equal amount of force to balance this in the opposite direction. In this case, that reaction results in the forward motion of the aircraft or rocket.

Here's how to make a simple demonstration of the third law with a drinking straw, a balloon, some tape, and a ball of string. Tie one end of a long piece of string to something

The canoeist's action as he pushes the water backward with his paddle creates the reaction of the canoe's forward motion.

sturdy. Tie it well above ground level. A tree trunk, lamp-post, or doorknob will work well. Slip the string through a plastic drinking straw, pull the string tight, and tie the other end to another sturdy object. The string should be tight enough that it doesn't sag in the middle. Slide the straw to one end of the string. Next, inflate the balloon and close off the end with a short piece of string tied in a bow. Securely tape the inflated balloon to the straw, with the tied end of the balloon facing the end of the string. Untie the bow holding the air in the balloon and watch your rocket take off.

Why does this work? The air escaping from the balloon exerts a force. That is the action from Newton's third law. The balloon "rocket" moves forward along the string in the opposite direction, as a reaction to that force.

Perhaps you've seen plastic toy rockets that are designed to be filled with water and then pumped up with air pressure. When they are released, the air pressure forces

When you untie the bow, the balloon rocket will travel along the string.

the water out the back of the rocket. The rocket leaps into the air as the water jets out the back. Of course, this toy works because of Newton's third law.

Can you figure out why this kind of water rocket goes much farther than an air-powered balloon rocket? It's because of Newton's second law. Water has much more mass than air. When the water accelerates out the back of the rocket, it creates much more force than the small amount of air would. The reaction to that force sends the water rocket soaring.

The third law is even at work when we walk down the street. Imagine what it would be like if, when we pushed against the Earth with our feet, nothing pushed back. With no resistance, we'd never get anywhere! Fortunately, when we push against the Earth with our feet, we do get resistance. Our muscles push against the Earth (action), and our body moves forward (reaction).

Newton's three laws of motion were first published in 1687 in the book *Mathematical Principles of Natural Philosophy*. This book, usually known as the *Principia* (pronounced "prihn-KIHP-ee-uh"), is one of the most important and influential books ever written. Along with the laws of motion, it also describes Newton's law of gravitation, which you will read about in the next chapter.

In addition to his discoveries about motion and gravitation, Newton also made important discoveries about light. He also invented a new kind of mathematics called calculus. Newton received many honors for his discoveries. The metric unit used to measure force, called the newton, was named in his honor.

Scientists and philosophers of his time were tremendously excited by Newton's laws. They began to think that the universe worked like a huge but predictable machine. Some scientists thought that if they could just measure all the forces and masses of objects moving through the universe, they could predict exactly what the results of any event would be. It wasn't until the twentieth century that Albert Einstein showed that even Newton's laws, great as they were, couldn't describe everything that happens in our amazing universe.

CHAPTER

Since the earliest times, people have known that objects that are dropped or thrown will fall back to the Earth. The familiar saying, "What goes up must come down," is not the law of gravity. Isaac Newton's great discovery was that gravitation is a universal force. The force of gravity exists in every corner of the universe. It works the same way everywhere. Isaac Newton didn't discover gravity. He discovered that a single force is responsible for the motions of the planets, the Moon, the Sun, the tides, and falling objects. That is why his discovery is properly known as the *law of universal gravitation*.

When he was a young man, Newton wondered why the Moon endlessly circles the Earth. As he sat in his mother's orchard and watched an apple fall to the ground, he suddenly realized that the same force that caused this ordinary event must hold the Moon in its orbit.

The law of universal gravitation is stated this way: Any

two objects attract each other with a force that is directly proportional to the product of their masses and inversely proportional to the square of the distance between their centers. Let's take this statement one phrase at a time and see exactly what it means.

"Any two objects attract each other . . . " means that the law of gravitation applies to any object in the universe. It applies to apples, rocks, people, spacecraft, planets, and stars. Every object in the universe has gravitational attraction for all other objects.

But if that is true, why don't we see objects like apples or rocks pulling toward one another all the time? It is because the force of gravity is a very weak force. It is so weak that we only notice it in very massive objects, like the Earth.

Even a huge object like a skyscraper doesn't exert enough gravitational force for us to feel. Compared to the pull of the Earth itself, its gravitational pull is unnoticeable. Although sensitive instruments can measure the gravitational pull of a giant office building, we can walk past it without feeling a thing. Even our own muscle power is strong enough to let us temporarily lift our bodies away from the gravitation of the huge Earth, whenever we walk, run, or jump. Nevertheless, every object in the universe, from the largest galaxy to the smallest atom, exerts some gravitational force.

Objects attract each other "with a force that is directly proportional to the product of their masses . . . ." Remember what directly proportional means? As one measurement increases, the other increases as well. In the case of the law of universal gravitation, when the masses of objects increase, the gravitational force between them increases too. Mass is the amount of matter an object is made of. To calculate the attraction between any two objects, the product of their masses must be calculated. That means that the two masses must be multiplied. Because of that, if one object is twice as large as another, it exerts twice as much gravitational force.

One of the things that made Newton's law of universal gravitation such an important discovery was that it explained so many different things. One of the things it explained was Galileo's law of uniform acceleration.

Think about the attraction between the Earth and a cannonball with a mass of 10 kilograms (22 pounds). If we double the amount of mass to 20 kilograms (44 pounds), the law of universal gravitation tells us that the attraction between the Earth and the cannonball will be twice as much. But if that is true, why doesn't the larger cannonball fall twice as fast as the smaller one? Remember, Galileo proved that objects on Earth fall at the same rate.

The answer comes from Newton's second law of motion. That law says that acceleration increases as the amount of force increases. But acceleration also decreases as the amount of mass increases. Gravity is pulling the larger cannonball with twice as much force. But the cannonball also has twice as much mass to get moving. The effects of the change in force and the change in mass cancel each other out. So both cannonballs fall at exactly the same rate!

Let's look at the final part of the law: "and inversely proportional to the square of the distance between their centers." Remember that when two measurements are inversely proportional, one amount decreases as the other amount increases. In the law of universal gravitation, as the distance between two objects increases, the amount of gravitational force decreases.

Gravitational force decreases by the square of the distance between the two objects. When you square a number, you multiply it by itself. The square of 2 is 2×2, or 4; the square of 3 is 3×3, or 9. The symbol used to indicate that a number is squared is a small 2 placed at the upper right of the number. That 2 is called an exponent. It tells you how many times to multiply the bigger number by itself. It looks like this:

$$5^2 = 25$$

The law of universal gravitation says that if the distance between two objects is doubled, there is only one-fourth as much gravitational attraction between them. If the distance is tripled, there is only one-ninth as much gravitational attraction.

This relationship is called an *inverse square law*. Gravitation is only one of many forces in nature that work according to an inverse square relationship. Other things that follow inverse square laws include light, magnetism, and electrical force. An explanation of why gravity and other forces follow this rule begins on page 62.

Notice that the law of universal gravitation measures gravitational force from the centers of objects. Newton found that the force of gravitation acts as if it is concentrated at the center of each object. Of course, the Earth's gravity doesn't come only from its center. Earth's gravity comes from its entire mass. But gravity acts as if it comes from the center of the Earth. That's why objects fall "down" toward the center of the Earth whether they are in the United States, Australia, Japan, France, or the South Pole.

Mathematically, the law of universal gravitation looks like this:

$$\frac{\text{force of}}{\text{gravitation}} = \frac{\text{gravitational}}{\text{constant}} \times \frac{\text{mass (1)} \times \text{mass (2)}}{\text{distance}^2}$$

or

$$F = G \times \frac{m(1) \times m(2)}{d^2}$$

In this equation, F stands for gravitational force, $m(1)$ and $m(2)$ stand for the masses of the two objects attracting each other, and *d* stands for the distance between them. *G* is a special, very small number called the gravitational constant. This constant allows scientists to calculate the exact force between any two objects.

Scientists in Newton's day didn't have equipment that could measure the precise value of *G*. But in 1798, the English scientist Henry Cavendish built a very sensitive device that could. Cavendish mounted a lead ball on each end of a long rod. The rod was hung on a very fine wire. Cavendish then moved two larger lead balls near the two balls on his instrument. The balls on the hanging rod were attracted to the other balls by gravitation. This caused the rod and wire to twist slightly. Cavendish measured the amount of twist.

Since he already knew the masses of the lead balls, Cavendish could calculate the exact strength of the attraction that produced the twist in the wire. Then he calculated the gravitational constant, *G*. Cavendish also used his experiment to compute the mass of the Earth for the first time. It turned out that the Earth has a mass of about 6 septillion (6,000,000,000,000,000,000,000,000) kilograms (13 septillion pounds).

In the *Principia*, Newton explained how gravitation causes the Moon to orbit around the Earth. Because of gravitation, the Moon always falls toward the Earth. But the Moon is also moving forward through space. The Moon's inertia (Newton's first law of motion) keeps it moving away from the Earth in a straight line. So as the Moon falls toward the Earth, it also travels far enough to move past it. The Moon is constantly "falling around" the Earth. This is called free fall. Any spacecraft with enough speed can orbit the Earth in just the same way. The two forces—gravity and the motion of inertia—balance exactly, keeping the Moon and the Earth's artificial satellites in their regular orbits.

Newton's law of universal gravitation also explained Kepler's laws of planetary motion. The planets fall around the Sun just as the Moon falls around the Earth. Newton's law says that the closer two objects are to each other, the stronger the gravitational attraction the two objects have for each other. So when a planet is in the part of its orbit closest to the Sun, gravitation pulls more strongly on it, and it moves faster. In the farthest part of its orbit, the gravitational pull is weaker, and so it accelerates less. That is just what Kepler's second law of planetary motion describes.

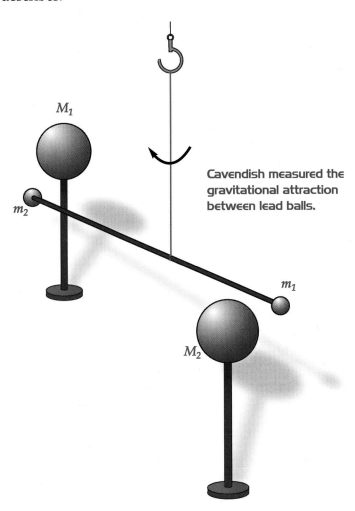

Cavendish measured the gravitational attraction between lead balls.

forward

resulting orbit

gravity

Our Moon's orbit is a balance of gravitational attraction to Earth and the Moon's own inertia (motion).

Kepler discovered that planets farther out in the solar system move more slowly than those nearer to the Sun (Kepler's third law of planetary motion). Newton's law explains this. The farther away from the Sun a planet is, the weaker the force of gravitation. Less gravitational force means less acceleration is needed to keep the planet in a regular orbit.

Newton showed that tides are caused by the gravitational pull of the Moon and the Sun on bodies of water. The law of universal gravitation even helped astronomers discover new planets!

The planet Uranus was discovered in 1781. But astronomers noticed that its orbit had a slight wobble. They realized that some undiscovered planet beyond it must be pulling Uranus with gravitational force. Using Newton's law, two astronomers calculated where they thought the planet ought to be. In 1846, another astronomer pointed his telescope toward that spot in the sky. Sure enough, there was the planet Neptune. In 1930, the planet Pluto was discovered in a similar way.

Newton's description of the law of universal gravitation also shows the difference between mass and weight. Mass is the amount of matter that makes up an object. Weight is a measure of the amount of gravitational pull on that mass.

As a simple example, imagine weighing yourself on the Earth and on the Moon. Of course, you will weigh much more under the Earth's gravity than you will under the Moon's gravity. If you weigh 100 pounds (45 kilograms) on the Earth, you will weigh only about 18 pounds (8 kilograms) on the Moon. That is because the Earth is much more massive than the Moon. The Earth has much more gravitational pull. However, your body still has the same amount of mass in either place.

When he wrote the *Principia*, Newton suggested an idea that was three hundred years ahead of its time. Newton had his readers imagine an extremely high mountain. The mountain would be so high that the top would be above the Earth's atmosphere. On the top of that mountain, Newton imagined a very powerful cannon. As the cannon was loaded with larger and larger charges of powder, its shots would travel farther and farther before they finally fell to the Earth. If the force of the cannon were strong enough,

Newton said, the cannonball would travel fast enough to fall completely around the Earth. Since there would be no air resistance to slow the cannonball as it fell, it would be launched into orbit! Of course, in the 1600s there was no way this could be done. But three centuries later, rocket engines were powerful enough to launch a projectile through the atmosphere and into orbit around the Earth.

Let's look at a voyage of the space shuttle once more. The space shuttle on its launchpad has a tremendous amount of mass. Since it is standing still, it has a tremendous amount of inertia to overcome in order to get moving. Remember that an object at rest continues at rest until acted upon by a force (Newton's first law of motion).

The force to overcome that inertia and blast the shuttle into orbit comes from the rocket engines. The blast of the engines forces hot gases backward out of the rockets. As a reaction to this thrust of gases, the shuttle lifts off the pad and gradually picks up speed. For every action there is an equal, opposite reaction (Newton's third law of motion).

With the rocket engines providing the force for the shuttle's acceleration, the spacecraft goes faster and faster. And as the rockets burn their fuel, the launch vehicle gets lighter and lighter, and the engines can accelerate it even faster. Remember that the acceleration of an object is inversely proportional to the mass of the object and directly proportional to the force applied to it (Newton's second law of motion).

Finally, the shuttle is moving fast enough, at a distance far enough from the Earth, to put it into orbit. The Earth's gravity pulls the shuttle back toward the center of the Earth. But the shuttle has enough forward motion to fall around the Earth in continuous free fall. Any two objects attract each other with a force that is directly proportional to the product of their masses and inversely proportional to the square of the distance between their centers (Newton's law of universal gravitation).

It's amazing that Newton's discoveries still apply today, three hundred years after the *Principia* was first printed. It shows us how important Newton's laws are in our lives and how great an achievement his discoveries were. Very few human accomplishments last that long.

CHAPTER 5

Conservation of Momentum

Picture two balls moving in the same direction at a speed of 1 meter (3 feet) per second. One is a 5-gram (0.2-ounce) table-tennis ball and the other is a 5-kilogram (11-pound) bowling ball. They both have the same velocity. But can we say that they have the same amount of motion?

What would happen if both balls were to collide with something, like an array of bowling pins? The table-tennis ball would just bounce off the pins and fly off in a new direction. But the bowling ball would slam into the pins, knocking them down as it continued on its way. Even though the velocities of the two balls were the same, the bowling ball certainly would have much more total motion.

How can we measure exactly how much motion a moving object has? Knowing its velocity tells us its speed and direction. But we also need to know how large it is. We must know both its velocity and its mass.

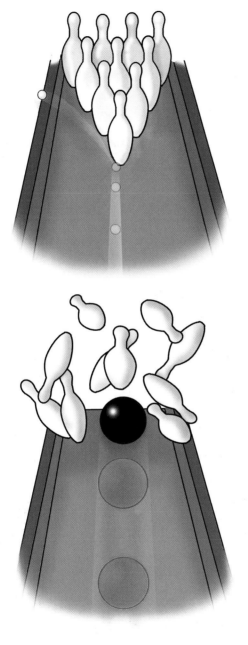

A table-tennis ball and a bowling ball traveling at the same speed will have very different effects on a set of bowling pins.

The word for the total amount of motion of an object is momentum. Scientists actually recognize two different kinds of momentum. One is linear momentum, or momentum in a straight line. The second kind of momentum is called angular momentum. That is the momentum of spinning objects.

Multiplying the mass of an object by its velocity gives us the total amount of linear momentum of an object. The mathematical equation for momentum is:

$$\text{momentum} = \text{mass} \times \text{velocity} \quad \text{or} \quad p = m \times v$$

In our example, the 5-gram table-tennis ball is moving at 1 meter (3 feet) per second. To calculate its momentum, we multiply the mass times the velocity. So the momentum of the table-tennis ball is 5 gram-meters per second.

Let's do the same with the 5-kilogram bowling ball. We multiply its mass times the velocity. Since 5 kilograms equals 5,000 grams (11 pounds) the momentum of the bowling ball is 5,000 gram-meters per second. Both balls are moving at the same velocity, but the bowling ball has one thousand times more momentum.

Think about what happens in a collision between a moving vehicle and a stationary object like a brick wall. The larger a vehicle is, the more momentum it has. And the faster a vehicle is moving, the more momentum it has. That's why the amount of damage in a crash depends on both the size and the speed of the vehicle.

A large vehicle will do much more damage as it crashes into a wall than a smaller one. The larger vehicle has more mass and thus more momentum. Similarly, a faster-moving vehicle will do more damage than a slower one. The faster vehicle has more momentum because it has more velocity.

Newton's first law of motion says that the motion of an object remains unchanged unless the object is acted upon by a force. So the momentum of an object must also remain unchanged. When a quantity always remains unchanged, scientists say that it is conserved. Unless an outside force acts on an object, its momentum is conserved. The Dutch scientist Christiaan Huygens was the first of many scientists to recognize and study this law.

What happens when two or more objects are involved in an event? Let's consider a collision between two billiard balls as an example. One ball is rolling toward a second ball that is standing still. The first ball has a certain amount of momentum, but the second has none. When they collide, the moving ball transfers some of its momentum to the stationary ball, and both balls roll off.

The momentum of the first ball is divided between the two moving balls. Each of the balls is rolling more slowly than the one ball was moving before the collision. If you add the momentum of the two balls after the collision, the total will equal the momentum of the one moving ball before the collision. The total amount of motion is conserved. Huygens and others realized that momentum is always conserved in any object or any interacting group of objects.

The *law of conservation of momentum* says that the total linear momentum of any object or system of objects remains constant, as long as no outside force acts upon the object or system. The objects in a system may move, collide, or fly apart, but their total momentum remains the same. The law of conservation of momentum applies to any object in motion, from an atom to a galaxy.

The effects of this law can be difficult to see in the real world. When we experiment with real balls, some of their momentum is absorbed by the surface they roll on. We have to remember that the ball is only part of a larger group of objects that include the Earth itself. The momentum of an object that rolls to a stop or bangs into a wall doesn't disappear. It is just transferred to another part of the system of objects. When a ball loses speed to friction or collides with an object that is firmly attached to the Earth, the Earth gains every bit of momentum that the ball loses. But the Earth is so massive that this tiny change in its momentum is completely unnoticeable.

For one more example of conservation of momentum, picture a loaded cannon mounted on wheels. The cannon is standing still. Its momentum is 0. Imagine that we fire the cannon. The cannonball flies out the barrel of the cannon, and the cannon recoils, rolling backward with the same amount of force.

Newton's third law of motion says that every action has an equal, opposite reaction. The cannonball and the cannon form a system of two objects moving in opposite directions with the same amount of force. If we add the momentum of the two objects together, the total amount of force in this system of objects is still 0! In fact, Newton's third law is just another way of stating the law of conservation of momentum.

We use our knowledge of momentum every day, without realizing it. Whenever we walk, run, or ride, we must constantly judge our own momentum to keep us from colliding into other people or objects. As you approach a stop sign on your bicycle, you must judge the momentum of the system of moving objects that includes both you and your moving bicycle. You apply pressure to the brakes according to that judgment. Fortunately, our brains have the ability to estimate our personal momentum very effectively, without a lot of mathematical calculation.

So far, we've looked at the momentum of objects in straight-line motion. But there is a second kind of momentum. Spin also gives an object a kind of momentum, which must be measured separately.

An object's rotation can be measured in revolutions per second. Picture our bowling ball and table-tennis ball again. Suppose they are both spinning at one revolution per second. Which ball would be easier to stop spinning?

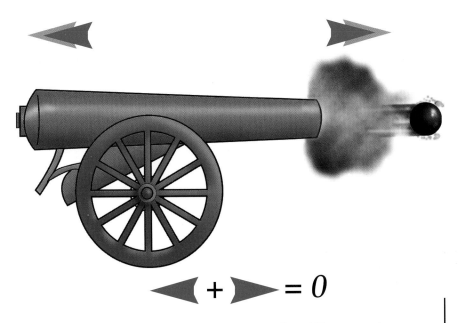

$$\blacktriangleleft + \blacktriangleright = 0$$

If you add the momentum of the cannonball and the momentum of the recoiling cannon, the total momentum is 0.

Obviously, the table-tennis ball could be stopped with much less force than the bowling ball. Even though they are both rotating at the same velocity, the bowling ball has a larger amount of spinning motion.

The amount of spinning motion that an object has is called angular momentum. It's called that because the spin of an object can be measured by measuring how quickly it rotates through the 360 degrees of a circle.

To measure angular momentum, we need to know how much mass an object has and how fast it is spinning. But calculating the angular momentum of an object is trickier than measuring its linear momentum. That's because different points on a spinning object move at different speeds.

Picture a disk with a radius of 3 centimeters (1.2 inches). That means it measures 3 centimeters from the center of the disk to the outside edge. Let's put marks at the center of the disk, and at 1, 2, and 3 centimeters (0.4, 0.8, 1.2 inches) from the center. Imagine that this disk is spinning at one revolution per second. Do each of the points we marked move the same distance in the same amount of time? Let's see.

In one second, each point revolves only once around the center of the disk. If we trace the path of each point as it turns, we see that each point traces a circle as it moves.

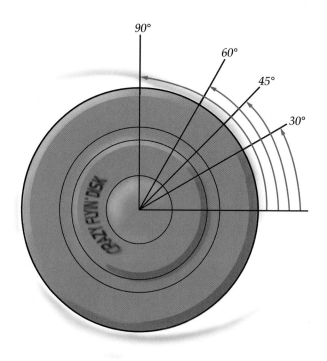

Momentum of spin is called angular momentum because the rotating object spins through a series of angles.

You can see that the outer point of the disk travels much farther in one second than the inner points. The whole disk is spinning at one revolution per second, but different places on the disk are moving at different speeds! Since the outer part of the disk is moving faster, it must generate more momentum than the inner part of the disk.

To compute the disk's momentum, we need to know more than just its mass and its rate of spin. We also need to know the radius, or the distance from the disk's center to its outer edge.

The angular momentum of a spinning object depends on three things: its mass, its rate of rotation, and its radius. Just as with linear momentum, the larger the mass or the faster the velocity, the more momentum a spinning object has. A spinning bowling ball has more angular momentum than a table-tennis ball spinning at the same rate. And a bowling ball spinning at two revolutions per second has twice as much momentum as the same ball spinning once per second.

Also, the farther the mass of a rotating object is from its center, the more angular momentum that object has. For example, our solar system is a rotating system of objects. It has an enormous amount of angular momentum, not just because the planets are so massive, but also because they are revolving so far from the center of spin.

The total amount of angular momentum of any object or group of objects is conserved. The law of conservation of momentum says that the total angular momentum of any spinning object or group of objects remains constant, as long as no outside force acts upon the object or system. Like conservation of linear momentum, this law applies to all objects, from atomic particles to spinning galaxies.

You can see conservation of angular momentum in the graceful spin of a figure skater. A skater starts a spin with his arms far away from his body. That puts his mass as far as possible from the center of spin. Once the skater is spinning, he pulls his arms close to his body. His mass is then much closer to the center of spin. His angular momentum must be conserved. Since his radius of spin is smaller, he must spin faster to keep the same amount of momentum. The next time you watch figure skating on television, you can see this happening.

When you pull the books closer to your body, your rate of spin increases, but your angular momentum remains the same.

You can experience conservation of momentum your-self with just a spinning stool and a couple of heavy books for extra mass. Sit on the stool and extend your arms, hold-ing the books out from your body. Have someone give you a spin. After you are spinning, bring your arms in close to your chest. To conserve your angular momentum, you will spin faster as you reduce your radius by pulling your arms in.

Frisbees, tops, and toy gyroscopes work because of angular momentum. When you throw a Frisbee or spin a top, you give the toy a lot of angular momentum. Its momentum can be changed only by an outside force, and the forces acting on the toy are comparatively weak: air resistance and friction. So the angular momentum makes the toy very stable.

Precise gyroscopes are used as navigation equipment in ships and missiles. These gyroscopes are large masses spin-ning very rapidly inside movable frames. The spinning gyroscope is set in a specific direction, such as due north. Its angular momentum keeps it pointing north, no matter what direction the vehicle may take. The exact direction that the vehicle is traveling can be calculated by comparing it to the direction of the spinning gyroscope.

An object can have either angular momentum or linear momentum or both. For example, the Earth is both spin-ning and moving through space. A Frisbee spins and flies at the same time too. The two kinds of momentum are clearly very similar to each other. Each depends on the amount of mass and the velocity of the object.

We can change one type of momentum into the other. For example, spinning lawn sprinklers change linear momentum into angular momentum. In a spinning sprinkler, each drop of water shoots out of the nozzle in a straight line: linear momentum. But the action also causes the sprinkler to react by moving backward. That motion spins the sprinkler around, giving it angular momentum.

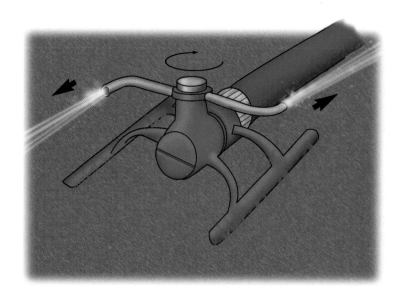

A garden sprinkler turns the linear motion of the spraying water into the rotating motion of the spinning sprinkler area.

It's just as easy to change angular momentum into linear momentum. Imagine a spinning rubber ball. If you were to touch the ball with a pencil, the spinning motion of the ball would be converted to straight-line motion, and the ball would rapidly roll away. Angular momentum would have become linear momentum.

In every event, large or small, that takes place in our universe, the total amount of motion must always be conserved. That is the law of conservation of momentum. So scientists know that whenever they observe and measure an event, they must account for all the momentum of the objects involved. If measurements show that some momentum seems to be missing, then researchers know that they have missed observing something and must look more carefully. Knowing this has led to several important discoveries, including the discovery of the subatomic particles called neutrinos and the discoveries of planets, stars, and black holes.

The law of conservation of momentum says that the momentum of any object or system of objects remains constant, as long as no outside force acts upon the object or system. If we consider the entire universe as a system of objects, then there are no outside forces. The universe includes everything there is. There is nothing outside it.

That means that the total amount of momentum in the universe must always remain constant. As galaxies collide, new stars form, and old stars explode, the total amount of motion in the universe will never change! Scientists believe that our universe was first created billions of years ago in a huge explosion they call the big bang. The same motion first created in the big bang is still with us today, spread among the vast number of stars, planets, atoms, and atomic particles moving and spinning through the cosmos.

We don't know all there is to know about the universe. Scientists still have much to learn about the stars and planets, the atom, and the miracles of life. There are still more laws to discover and more mysteries to solve. Perhaps you may one day add your name to that distinguished list of scientists who have helped to discover the secrets of the universe.

Inverse Square Laws

A number of important natural laws all follow a similar pattern. This pattern is known as an inverse square law. Gravitational force behaves in this way. So do electrical and magnetic forces. So does the intensity of light. It isn't an accident that all these laws are so similar. Here is an explanation of why inverse square laws apply to so many different kinds of forces.

In all inverse square laws, the strength of the force that the law describes is inversely proportional to the distance from the source of the force. When two quantities are inversely proportional, one measurement decreases as the other one increases. The intensity of a force decreases as the distance increases. In all inverse square laws, however, the intensity decreases in proportion to the *square* of the distance from the center of force.

The intensity of light follows an inverse square law. The intensity of light is inversely proportional to the square of the distance from the light source. As you get farther from a light source, the brightness of the light from that source decreases. Let's use light as an example to see why so many different forces follow this one pattern.

Imagine a source of light such as a tiny electric bulb in the middle of a large, dark space. The light spreads out from the source in all directions, like an expanding bubble. Light intensity is measured in lumens. Let's suppose our light source is producing a total of 1,000 lumens of light.

Picture a sphere with a 1-meter radius surrounding the light source. The light from the source illuminates the inside of the sphere. How much area does the light have to illuminate? The surface area (A) of a sphere is calculated by multiplying 4 times π (pi, or 3.14) times the square of the radius (r) of the sphere.

$$A = 4 \times \pi \times r^2$$

So our sphere has a surface area of 12.6 square meters (136 square feet). The 1,000 lumens of light produced by the bulb will be distributed evenly around those 12.6 square meters of surface.

Dividing the total amount of light by the number of square meters in the sphere will tell us how much light is shining on each square meter. When we divide 1,000 lumens among 12.6 square meters, we find that each square meter is illuminated with about 80 lumens of light.

Suppose we double the radius of the sphere surrounding our light source. You will see that the 1,000 lumens of light get distributed over a much larger area. The new sphere has a radius of 2 meters. To compute the total surface area, again we multiply $4 \times \pi \times r^2$. Our new sphere has an area of 50.2 square meters (540 square feet). The radius of the new sphere is only twice the radius of the first sphere. But the area of the second sphere is four times the area of the first. That is because the area of a sphere is based on the square of the radius.

Our light source is still producing the same amount of light: 1,000 lumens. But at this distance, that same amount of light is shining on a sphere with 50.2 square meters of area. So each square meter receives only about 20 lumens of light. This is only one-fourth the amount of light that each square meter received in the first sphere. The distance from the light source to the sphere has doubled, but the intensity of the light is only one-fourth as great. This is an inverse square relationship.

The same thing holds true if the radius is increased to 3 meters. Once again we multiply $4 \times \pi \times r^2$. Our third sphere has a surface area of 113.04 square meters (1216.8 square feet). The radius of this sphere is three times as big as the radius of the original sphere, but the area of the third sphere is nine times larger. Our 1,000 lumens of light are spread out across 113 square meters of area. Each square meter of our third sphere receives about 9 lumens of light.

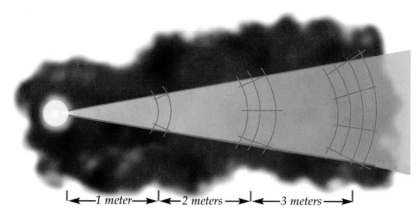

|←—1 meter—→|←—2 meters—→|←—3 meters—→|

The same amount of light, as it spreads out from a source, fills an increasingly large area.

This is only one-ninth of the amount each square meter received in the first sphere. The distance from the center to the sphere has now tripled, but the intensity of the light is only one-ninth as great.

Of course, the spheres don't actually exist. The imaginary spheres simply give us a way of picturing why the intensity of the light decreases at a much quicker rate than the distance increases. It's because the total amount of energy gets spread out over a rapidly expanding area.

You should even be able to see this inverse square law happening with your own eyes. Mark off distances of 10, 20, and 30 meters (30, 60, and 90 feet) from a 0 point in your backyard or on the sidewalk near your house. When it gets dark, stand on your 0 point. Ask someone to stand with a flashlight on the 10-meter mark. Look at the intensity of the light. Have the person move to the 20-meter mark and then the 30-meter mark, and compare what you see. Although you won't be able to measure the intensity unless you have a very sensitive light meter, you should be able to tell that it is decreasing rapidly as your assistant moves farther away.

You can picture gravitational force spreading out from the center of the Earth (or any other mass) in the same way that light spreads out from a light source. You can picture a magnetic or electrical field spreading outward from a source in a similar way. Picture each force spreading outward from its source like an ever-expanding bubble. Inverse square relationships hold true for all these forces because they all spread out evenly in all directions from the center point at which they are generated. As you get farther and farther away from the center point, the effect of these forces is spread over a much larger area.

c. 343 B.C.   Aristotle becomes Alexander the Great's tutor

c. 300 B.C.   Euclid's *Elements* establishes basic geometry

c. 287 B.C.   Archimedes' birth

240 B.C.   Chinese astronomers observe the comet that will eventually be named Halley's comet

c. A.D. 150   **Ptolemy of Alexandria presents an Earth-centered model of the universe**

c. 1455   Johannes Gutenberg prints the Bible using movable type

1492   Christopher Columbus makes his first voyage of discovery

1503   Leonardo da Vinci paints the *Mona Lisa*

1517   Martin Luther posts his 95 Theses on the church door in Wittenberg, Germany

1519   Ferdinand Magellan begins his expedition to circumnavigate the globe

1543   Nicolaus Copernicus's *On the Revolution of the Heavenly Spheres* is published

1560   Partial solar eclipse occurs and is observed by Tycho Brahe

1581   **Galileo conducts pendulum experiments**

1609   **Johannes Kepler publishes the first two laws of planetary motion**

1620   The *Mayflower* lands in Massachusetts

1633	Galileo is condemned by the Inquisition and placed under house arrest
1657	**Christiaan Huygens patents his first pendulum clock**
1668	Sir Isaac Newton makes the first reflecting telescope
1687	**Sir Isaac Newton publishes his *Principia***
1692	Witchcraft trials take place in Salem, Massachusetts
1776	American Declaration of Independence is written
1781	**Discovery of the planet Uranus**
1789	George Washington becomes the first president of the United States
1798	**Henry Cavendish measures the mass and density of the Earth using the gravitational constant (*G*)**
1829	Louis Braille's system of writing for the blind is first published (revised in 1837)
1846	**Discovery of the planet Neptune**
1861–1865	American Civil War
1865	President Abraham Lincoln is assassinated
1876	Alexander Graham Bell patents the telephone
1903	The Wright brothers make the first manned airplane flight
1905	Albert Einstein publishes his special theory of relativity, including $E=mc^2$
1908	Henry Ford begins production of the Model T
1930	**Discovery of the planet Pluto**

Archimedes
(c. 287–212 B.C.)

was a mathematician and physicist from Syracuse, a Greek colony in Sicily. His many discoveries and inventions and his work in mathematics make him one of the most important figures in early science. The compound pulley and the principle of the lever are two of his major contributions. He may be best known for discovering—supposedly while in the bathtub—the law of buoyancy, also known as Archimedes' principle. Little is known about Archimedes' personal life. The son of an astronomer named Phidias, he was probably introduced to science and mathematics at a young age. Toward the end of his life, Archimedes created many inventive weapons to defend Syracuse against Roman invaders. The stories of these weapons describe giant mirrors that were used to set ships on fire and a "claw" that lifted ships and turned them over or crushed them against rocks. These tales are almost surely exaggerations, but it is likely that Archimedes invented the catapult. When Syracuse was finally captured, Archimedes was killed by a Roman soldier. Legends say that he was working a geometry problem in the sand and made the soldier angry by telling him, "Do not disturb my circles."

Aristotle
(384–322 B.C.)

was a Greek philosopher and scientist. He was born in Stagira, Macedonia (part of Greece), where his father was the king's doctor. As a young man, Aristotle moved to Athens to study at Plato's Academy. He was one of Plato's best students, and he later became young Alexander the Great's tutor. After a few years of travel, Aristotle returned to Athens and started his own school, the Lyceum. During his lifetime, Aristotle wrote and lectured on the subjects of logic, ethics, politics, psychology, biology, zoology, physics, and astronomy. Some of these fields were quite new at the time, and many people consider Aristotle the founder of the natural sciences. Though some of his theories were later proven to be incorrect, such as the idea that heavy objects fall faster than light ones, Aristotle was very important in establishing the basic principles of scientific observation.

Tycho Brahe **(A.D. 1546–1601)** was a Danish scientist. When he was fourteen years old, he witnessed a partial solar eclipse. Although Brahe was pressured by his family to become a politician, he chose to become an astronomer instead. Brahe spent more than twenty years carefully observing and measuring the movements of more than seven hundred stars. He did all of this without the use of a telescope, which had not yet been invented. He did, however, use and design many other instruments of astronomical observation. Toward the end of his life, Brahe also had the assistance of the young Johannes Kepler, who published their catalog of stars after Brahe's death. In addition to his great intelligence and his dedication to astronomy, Brahe is remembered for his eccentricity. At the age of nineteen, he lost part of his nose in a duel over mathematics and wore a false nose made of silver for the rest of his life!

Henry Cavendish **(1731–1810)** was a British chemist and physicist. One of the most brilliant scientists of his day, he was a shy and reclusive person who avoided personal contact. Though he occasionally joined fellow scientists in discussions about their work, he was quiet and uncomfortable in most social situations, especially around women. He came from a wealthy family and inherited a large fortune at age forty, but he spent little of his money on anything other than his research and books. His clothes were unfashionable and out of date, and he never entertained guests. However, Cavendish's studies kept him busy enough. Among other things, he proved that water is not an element, measured the density of the Earth, and determined the gravitational constant (*G*).

Nicolaus Copernicus (1473–1543) was a Polish astronomer, medical practitioner, and church official. His family's wealth gave him the freedom to attend schools in both Poland and Italy. He studied a wide variety of subjects, from languages and painting to medicine and law. But it was in the field of astronomy that he really made his mark. He caused quite a stir by suggesting the heliocentric (Sun-centered) model of the solar system. It certainly was a revolutionary idea to his contemporaries; a geocentric model, in which the Sun and planets orbit Earth, had been accepted for over 1,300 years. *On the Revolution of the Heavenly Spheres,* Copernicus's book describing his theory, was officially published in 1543, the year of his death. In 1616, the Catholic Church banned the work, and it remained on its "Index of Forbidden Books" until 1835.

Albert Einstein (1879–1955) was a German physicist. As a student, he enjoyed reading but disliked lectures and tests, and he was never a particular favorite with his teachers. His undistinguished university record led him to a job as a clerk in a Swiss patent office. From these modest beginnings, Einstein went on to introduce the special and general theories of relativity, changing the world of physics forever. And that wasn't all. Einstein published many other papers on topics such as the nature of light, molecular motion, and gravity. He traveled widely, giving lectures all over the world. As an international figure, Einstein was named a public enemy by the Nazis in Germany, acted as an unofficial adviser to U.S. president Franklin D. Roosevelt on the threat of the atomic bomb, and was even offered the presidency of Israel. In his private life, however, he had simple, quiet tastes. His hobbies included playing the violin and sailing.

Galileo Galilei (1564–1642) was born in Pisa, Italy. Although his father was a musician, Galileo's family hoped that he would become a doctor. He did study medicine at the University of Pisa for a little while, but he was more deeply interested in physics and mathematics. He was especially fascinated by pendulums and studied their movement in detail. In the early 1600s, his attention turned to astronomy. He built improved telescopes to investigate the stars and planets. His discoveries included four of Jupiter's moons and the phases of Venus. Galileo was one of the first scientists to regard experimentation and calculation as necessary companions to observation. Using these tools, he made discoveries that often contradicted long-accepted beliefs, bringing him into conflict with other scientists as well as with the Catholic Church. For example, he made important but controversial strides with his inclined-plane experiments, which disproved Aristotle's theory that heavy objects fall faster than light ones. A more dramatic conflict was caused by his support of the Copernican heliocentric model of the solar system. Galileo was tried by the Inquisition in 1633 and sentenced by the Church to house arrest.

Christiaan Huygens (1629–1695) was born to a wealthy Dutch family in The Hague. Educated in science and mathematics, he was one of many physicists to be puzzled and intrigued by the nature of light. In 1678, Huygens proposed his wave theory of light, which was contrary to the particle theory supported by Newton. Not until well after both their deaths would the dual nature of light be discovered. Another of Huygens's great contributions to physics was his study of the pendulum and its applications to timekeeping and clocks. Huygens had a strong interest in astronomy. His homemade telescope was a considerable improvement over those used by earlier scientists. With this telescope, he discovered Saturn's largest moon and more clearly distinguished the shape of Saturn's rings, which were first observed by Galileo. Huygens also had many theories regarding extraterrestrial life and wrote one of the earliest published works on the subject.

Johannes Kepler (1571–1630) was a German physicist and astronomer. He was a young theology student when a professor introduced him to the work of Copernicus. Fascinated by astronomy, he got the chance of a lifetime when he was invited to be Tycho Brahe's assistant. After Brahe's death in 1601, Kepler continued the work they had done together. Relying heavily on Brahe's hundreds of measurements, he discovered the three laws of planetary motion. These laws offered solid mathematical support of the Copernican heliocentric model of the solar system. In addition to his scientific interest in the stars and planets, Kepler also had a mystical interest. He was greatly intrigued by horoscopes and other aspects of astrology. But he was careful to point out a distinction between astrology and astronomy. Kepler, whose own eyesight was poor because of a childhood illness, also studied optics and human vision. He made important discoveries about the way lenses work, both in human-made tools such as eyeglasses and telescopes and in the human eye.

Sir Isaac Newton (1642–1727) was born in Woolsthorpe, England. His father, who died a few months before Newton's birth, was a farmer. Newton dutifully tried his hand at running the family farm, but his talents clearly lay elsewhere. Newton was a brilliant mathematician and scientist. Just a few of his many important contributions to science include the law of universal gravitation, the three laws of motion, the basic elements of calculus, and the particle theory of light. He also discovered the colored spectrum of white light. His book *Principia*, published in 1687, is one of the great masterpieces of science writing. Newton was also appointed as the Warden and later the Master of the Mint, and in 1705 he was knighted by the queen. He was an unconventional scholar who didn't care much how he looked and was notoriously absentminded. He has often been described as moody and withdrawn, and he had a tendency to get into bitter arguments with other scientists. Late in his life, Newton worked less on scientific and mathematical matters, turning instead to the study of alchemy, theology, and history.

Asimov, Isaac. *Asimov's Chronology of Science and Discovery.* New York: HarperCollins, 1994.

Friedhoffer, Robert. *Physics Lab in the Home.* New York: Franklin Watts, 1997.

Henderson, Harry, and Lisa Yount. *The Scientific Revolution.* San Diego: Lucent Books, 1996.

Hightower, Paul. *Galileo: Astronomer and Physicist.* Springfield, NJ: Enslow Publishers, Inc., 1997.

Lafferty, Peter. *Force and Motion.* New York: Dorling Kindersley, 1992.

Lampton, Christopher. *Astronomy: From Copernicus to the Space Telescope.* New York: Franklin Watts, 1987.

Meadows, Jack. *The Great Scientists.* New York: Oxford University Press, 1997.

Spangenburg, Ray. *The History of Science from the Ancient Greeks to the Scientific Revolution.* New York: Facts on File, 1993.

Wilkinson, Philip, and Michael Pollard. *Scientists Who Changed the World.* New York: Chelsea House Publishers, 1994.

Wood, Robert W. *Who?: Famous Experiments for the Young Scientist.* Philadelphia: Chelsea House Publishers, 1999.

Websites

Center for History of Physics, sponsored by the American
Institute of Physics
<http://www.aip.org/history/index.html>

Cool Science, sponsored by the U.S. Department of Energy
<http://www.fetc.doe.gov/coolscience/index.html>

The Franklin Institute Science Museum online
<http://www.fi.edu/tfi/welcome.html>

Kid's Castle, sponsored by the Smithsonian Institution.
Includes a science site.
<http://www.kidscastle.si.edu/>

NPR's *Sounds Like Science* site
<http://www.npr.org/programs/science/>

PBS's *A Science Odyssey* site
<http://www.pbs.org/wgbh/aso/>

Science Learning Network
<http://www.sln.org/>

Science Museum of Minnesota
<http://www.smm.org/>

For Further Reading

Adler, Irving. *The Wonders of Physics: An Introduction to the Physical World*. New York: Golden Press, 1966.

Asimov, Isaac. *Asimov's New Guide to Science*. New York: Basic Books, 1984.

_____. *The History of Physics*. New York: Walker and Co., 1966.

_____. *The Story of Gravity*. New York: E. P. Dutton, 1968.

Gamow, George. *Biography of Physics*. New York: Harper & Row, 1961.

Goldstein-Jackson, Kevin. *Experiments with Everyday Objects: Science Activities for Children, Parents and Teachers*. Englewood Cliffs, NJ: Prentice-Hall, 1978.

Kent, Amanda, and Alan Ward. *Introduction to Physics*. Tulsa, OK: Usborne Publishing, Ltd., 1983.

Millar, David, Ian Millar, John Millar, and Margaret Millar. *The Cambridge Dictionary of Scientists*. New York: Cambridge University Press, 1996.

Narlikar, Jayant V. *The Lighter Side of Gravity*. New York: W. H. Freeman, 1982.

Nourse, Alan E. *Universe, Earth, and Atom: The Story of Physics*. New York: Harper & Row, 1969.

Sagan, Carl. *Cosmos*. New York: Random House, 1980.

Silverberg, Robert. *Four Men Who Changed the Universe*. New York: G. P. Putnam's Sons, 1968.

Sullivan, Walter. *Black Holes*. New York: Anchor/Doubleday, 1979.

Westphal, Wilhelm H. *Physics Can Be Fun*. Alexandria, VA: Hawthorne Books, 1965.

Wilson, Mitchell. *Seesaws to Cosmic Rays: A First View of Physics*. New York: Lothrop, Lee & Shepard, 1967.

acceleration: any change in the motion of an object

gravitation, law of universal: any two objects attract each other with a force that is directly proportional to the product of their masses and inversely proportional to the square of the distance between their centers

momentum: total amount of motion of an object

momentum, law of conservation of: the momentum of any object or system of objects remains constant, as long as no outside force acts upon the object or system

motion, first law of: an object in motion continues in motion and an object at rest remains at rest unless acted upon by a force. Also called the law of inertia.

motion, second law of: the acceleration of an object is directly proportional to the force applied to it and inversely proportional to its mass

motion, third law of: for every action, there is an equal and opposite reaction. Also called the law of action and reaction.

pendulum motion, law of: if a pendulum of a certain length always swings at the same rate, it can be used to keep time

planetary motion, first law of: planets travel around the Sun in elliptical orbits

planetary motion, second law of: an orbiting planet sweeps out equal areas in equal amounts of time

planetary motion, third law of: the square of the time of each planet's revolution is proportional to the cube of its average distance from the Sun

uniform acceleration, law of: falling objects accelerate at a uniform rate

About the Author

Paul Fleisher has written more than twenty books for young people and educators, including *Life Cycles of a Dozen Diverse Creatures*, the *Webs of Life* series, and *Brain Food*. His most recent books are *Gorillas* and *Ice Cream Treats: The Inside Scoop*. Paul is a regular contributor to *Technology and Learning* magazine. He has also created several pieces of educational software, including the award-winning *Perplexing Puzzles*.

Paul has taught in Programs for the Gifted in Richmond, Virginia, since 1978. He is also active in civic organizations that work for peace and social justice. In 1988, he received the Virginia Education Association's Award for Peace and International Relations, and in 1999 he was awarded the Thomas Jefferson Medal for Outstanding Contributions to Natural Science Education. In his spare time, you may find Paul walking through the woods, gardening, or fishing on the Chesapeake Bay. Paul and his wife, Debra Sims Fleisher, live in Richmond, Virginia.